MW00643140

TABLE
OF
CONTENTS

THE PREGAME MEAL

THE PREGAME STRETCH

INDEX

TAILGATING MADNESS

The Cook-Off Before the Kick-Off

Printed in the United States of America
by G&R Publishing Co.

Distributed By:

507 Industrial Street
Waverly, IA 50677

ISBN 1-56383-209-7
Item #7009

THE PREGAME MEAL

FAVORITE RECIPES

NOTES

_____

_____

_____

_____

_____

_____

_____

_____

_____

_____

_____

_____

_____

_____

_____

_____

_____

_____

_____

_____

_____

_____

_____

THE STARTING
LINE-UP

APPETIZERS

TOUCHDOWN MEXICAN DIP

Makes 8 to 10 servings

1 (15 oz.) can refried beans
1/4 C. prepared guacamole
1 (8 oz.) pkg. cream cheese, softened
1 env. taco seasoning
1/2 C. shredded Cheddar cheese

3 green onions, chopped
1 (4 oz.) can sliced black olives, drained
2 medium tomatoes, chopped

On an 8" serving plate or pie pan, layer ingredients. Start by spreading an even layer of refried beans over serving plate, followed by a layer of guacamole. In a small bowl, combine cream cheese and taco seasoning mix. Spread cream cheese mixture over guacamole, followed by an even layer of shredded Cheddar cheese. Sprinkle chopped green onions, drained black olives and chopped tomatoes over shredded Cheddar cheese. Cover with plastic wrap and refrigerate or chill in cooler until ready to serve. Serve with tortilla chips for dipping.

Turkey Fryer Hot Wings

Makes about 15 servings

1 large bottle cooking oil　　**1 C. liquid butter**
40 lbs. chicken wings　　　　**1 C. hot sauce**

Pour cooking oil into a turkey fryer bucket until bucket is half full. Heat turkey fryer to between 375° and 400°. Use long heavy plastic gloves and carefully place wings, one at a time, into the hot oil. Cook batches of wings until lightly browned and cooked throughout. Remove wings from fryer bucket and let drain in a metal basket. Meanwhile, in a medium bowl, combine liquid butter and hot sauce, mixing well. Place 1 dozen cooked chicken wings in a large plastic bowl with a lid. Add 1/4 to 1/3 cup of the sauce in bowl with wings. Place lid on bowl and shake until wings are evenly coated with sauce. Remove wings to a serving tray and repeat with remaining wings and sauce. Serve with Bleu Cheese Dressing or Home-Style Ranch Dressing (page 4).

Variations: For maple-flavored wings, add 1/2 bottle of maple syrup to sauce, before tossing with wings. To make barbecue wings, simply use barbecue sauce in place of butter and hot sauce.

3

BLEU CHEESE DRESSING

Makes 1 1/2 cups

1 C. mayonnaise
2 T. minced onions
1 T. minced garlic
1/4 C. fresh chopped
    parsley
1/2 C. sour cream

1 T. lemon juice
1 T. distilled white vinegar
1/4 C. crumbled blue
    cheese
Salt and pepper to taste

In a small bowl, combine mayonnaise, minced onions, minced garlic, chopped parsley, sour cream, lemon juice, vinegar and blue cheese. Mix well and season with salt and pepper to taste. Cover with plastic wrap and refrigerate or chill in cooler until ready to serve.

HOME-STYLE RANCH DRESSING

Makes 1 1/2 cups

1 C. buttermilk
1 1/4 C. mayonnaise

1 env. ranch dressing mix

In a small bowl, combine buttermilk, mayonnaise and ranch dressing mix. Mix until well blended. Cover with plastic wrap and refrigerate or chill in cooler until ready to serve.

GUACAMOLE

Makes 8 servings

3 avocados, peeled
   and pitted
1 small onion, finely
   chopped
4 cloves garlic, minced

1 medium tomato,
   chopped
3 T. lemon juice
1 small jalapeno pepper,
   chopped
Salt and pepper to taste

In a large bowl, place peeled and pitted avocados. Using a fork, mash avocados into a lumpy paste. Add chopped onion, garlic, tomato, lemon juice and jalapeno pepper. Mix well and season with salt and pepper to taste. Cover with plastic wrap and refrigerate or chill in cooler until ready to serve. Serve with tortilla chips for dipping.

ARTICHOKE DIP

Makes 8 to 10 servings

1/2 C. mayonnaise
2 (8 oz.) pkgs. cream
   cheese, softened
1 (14 oz.) can artichoke
   hearts, drained and
   chopped

1 (10 oz.) pkg. frozen
   chopped spinach,
   thawed and drained
1 C. grated Parmesan
   cheese
3 cloves garlic, minced
2 T. lemon juice

Preheat oven to 375°. Lightly grease a 9x13" baking dish and set aside. In a medium bowl, combine mayonnaise and cream cheese, mixing until blended and creamy. Add chopped artichoke hearts, drained spinach and Parmesan cheese. Mix well and stir in garlic and lemon juice. Spread mixture evenly into prepared baking dish. Cover and bake in oven for 20 minutes. Remove cover for final 5 minutes of baking time. Serve with bread cubes, crackers or tortilla chips for dipping.

Cheesy Puffed Olives

Makes 12 servings

2 C. shredded Cheddar
   cheese
1/2 C. butter
1 C. flour

Dash of Worcestershire
   sauce
1 (5 oz.) jar pitted green
   olives

Preheat oven to 400°. Lightly grease a baking sheet and set aside. In a small bowl, combine Cheddar cheese, butter, flour and Worcestershire sauce. Mix well until a dough forms. Roll pieces of dough into small balls and flatten each ball in palms of hands. Roll each circle of dough around 1 olive. Arrange wrapped olives on prepared baking sheet. Bake in oven for 15 minutes, until lightly browned.

Easy Garlic Salsa

Makes 4 servings

1 (14 1/2 oz.) can diced
   tomatoes, drained
1/2 C. olive oil

1 T. minced garlic
1 T. fresh chopped parsley
Salt and pepper to taste

In a medium bowl, combine drained tomatoes, olive oil, minced garlic, chopped parsley, salt and pepper. Mix until well incorporated. Cover with plastic wrap and refrigerate or chill in cooler until ready to serve. Serve with tortilla chips for dipping.

SPINACH DIP IN A BREAD BOWL

Makes 10 servings

1 (10 oz.) pkg. frozen
   chopped spinach,
   drained
1 C. sour cream
1 C. mayonnaise
3/4 C. chopped green
   onions

2 tsp. dried parsley
   flakes
1 tsp. lemon juice
1/2 tsp. seasoning salt
1 (16 oz.) round loaf
   Hawaiian sweet bread

In a large bowl, combine drained spinach, sour cream, mayonnaise, chopped green onions, dried parsley flakes, lemon juice and seasoning salt. Mix until well blended and chill in refrigerator at least 1 hour. Cut a circle out of the top of the round bread loaf and scoop out the inside, leaving the outer shell of the loaf as a whole. Tear the inside pieces of the loaf into squares for dipping. Spoon chilled spinach dip into the center of the hollowed bread bowl and place on a serving platter. Place torn pieces of bread around bread bowl on platter. Encourage your fellow tailgaters to eat the bread bowl as well!

CHEDDAR BACON STUFFED MUSHROOMS

Makes 8 servings

3 slices bacon
8 large Crimini mushrooms
1 T. butter

1 T. chopped onions
3/4 C. shredded Cheddar cheese, divided

Preheat oven to 400°. In a large skillet over medium high heat, cook bacon slices until evenly browned. Remove bacon from skillet and let drain on paper towels. Finely dice the drained bacon. Remove stems from Crimini mushrooms and chop stems into pieces. Set mushroom caps aside. In a large saucepan over medium heat, place butter. Heat butter until melted and add chopped mushroom stems and chopped onions. Sauté mushrooms and onions until softened. Remove from heat and place sautéed mixture in a medium bowl. Add diced bacon and 1/2 cup shredded Cheddar cheese. Mix well and scoop mixture into mushroom caps. Place filled mushroom caps on an ungreased baking sheet. Bake in oven for 15 minutes, until cheese has melted. Remove mushrooms from oven and sprinkle with remaining 1/4 cup shredded Cheddar cheese.

PORK SPRING ROLLS

Makes 12 servings

1/2 lb. ground pork
1 C. finely shredded cabbage
1/4 C. finely shredded
   carrots
2 green onions, thinly sliced
2 T. fresh chopped cilantro
1/2 tsp. sesame oil
1/2 T. oyster sauce

2 tsp. fresh grated gingerroot
1 1/2 tsp. minced garlic
1 tsp. chile sauce
1 T. cornstarch
1 T. water
12 (7") square spring roll
   wrappers
4 tsp. vegetable oil

Preheat oven to 425°. In a medium saucepan over medium high heat, cook ground pork until evenly browned and cook throughout. Remove from heat and drain of fat. In a medium bowl, combine cooked pork, shredded cabbage, shredded carrots, sliced green onions, fresh chopped cilantro, sesame oil, oyster sauce, grated gingerroot, minced garlic and chile sauce. Mix until well combined. In a small bowl, combine cornstarch and water. Place about 1 tablespoon of the pork mixture in the center of each spring roll wrapper. Roll wrappers around mixture, folding edges in to enclose the filling. Moisten edges of spring roll wrappers with cornstarch mixture to seal. Place filled spring rolls in a single layer on an ungreased baking sheet. Brush spring rolls with vegetable oil and bake in oven for 20 minutes, until lightly browned. For crispy spring rolls, turn rolls after 10 minutes of baking time.

BROCCOLI BITES

Makes 2 dozen

3 T. Dijon mustard
4 T. honey
2 C. broccoli florets
1 C. shredded Cheddar
   cheese
1 egg

1 C. milk
1/2 C. flour
1/2 tsp. baking powder
1/2 tsp. salt
1/2 C. plus 1/2 tsp.
   vegetable oil, divided

In a small bowl, combine Dijon mustard and honey. Mix well and set aside. Chop broccoli florets into very small pieces and place in a medium bowl. Add shredded Cheddar cheese. Toss broccoli and cheese together and set aside. In a separate small bowl, combine egg and milk. Into a separate medium bowl, sift flour, baking powder and salt. Mix well and add egg and milk mixture. Add 1/2 teaspoon vegetable oil and pour mixture over broccoli and cheese mixture. Toss until evenly incorporated. In a large skillet or saucepan, heat remaining 1/2 cup vegetable oil to 375°. Drop broccoli mixture by small spoonfuls into hot oil and fry until golden brown. Remove with a slotted spoon to paper towels and let dry. Serve with Dijon mustard mixture as dipping sauce.

CRISPY BAKED ONION RINGS

Makes 4 to 6 servings

3 egg whites
2 large sweet onions,
    peeled and cut into
    1/4" slices
2 C. finely ground
    cornflakes crumbs

1/4 C. flour
2 tsp. chicken bouillon
1 tsp. chili powder

Preheat oven to 375°. In a large bowl, beat egg whites at medium high speed until foamy. Separate onion slices into individual rings. Place onion rings in bowl with egg whites and toss until evenly coated. In a separate bowl, combine cornflake crumbs, flour, chicken bouillon and chili powder. Mix well and pour mixture out onto a sheet of waxed paper. Roll the coated rings several times in the crumb mixture until onion rings have desired amount of coating. Place onion rings on a greased baking sheet. Bake in oven for 15 minutes, turning once, until coating is crispy and onions are softened.

Confetti Squares

Makes 35 (2"x2") squares

2 (8 oz.) pkgs. refrigerated crescent dinner rolls
2 (8 oz.) pkgs. cream cheese, softened
3 T. mayonnaise
1/2 tsp. dried basil
1/4 tsp. garlic powder

1 1/2 C. various chopped vegetables (green and red bell peppers, carrots, broccoli, onions)
2 T. McCormick Salad Supreme seasoning

Preheat oven to 350°. Unroll crescent dinner rolls into squares and press into the bottom and up sides of a 10x15" jellyroll pan. Bake in oven for 12 to 15 minutes. In a medium bowl, combine cream cheese, mayonnaise, dried basil and garlic powder. Mix until well blended. Spread an even thin layer of the cream cheese mixture over baked crust in pan. Place chopped vegetables over cream cheese layer and sprinkle a generous amount of Salad Supreme seasoning over vegetables. Cut into squares and place on a serving platter. Cover with plastic wrap and refrigerate or chill in cooler until ready to serve.

SPICY PARTY PRETZELS

Makes 15 servings

1 C. vegetable oil
1 (1 oz.) pkg. Ranch
   dressing mix
1 tsp. garlic salt

1 tsp. cayenne pepper
1 (15 oz.) pkg. mini twist
   pretzels

Preheat oven to 350°. In a medium bowl, combine vegetable oil, Ranch dressing mix, garlic salt and cayenne pepper. Stir until well mixed. Place pretzels in an even layer on a jellyroll pan and cover with vegetable oil mixture. Stir until evenly coated. Bake in oven for 1 hour, stirring occasionally to coat pretzels. Pretzels are done when toasted and crispy.

Fluffy Fruit Dip

Makes 12 to 16 servings

**1 (8 oz.) pkg. cream cheese,
    softened**

**1 (7 oz.) jar marshmallow
    crème**

In a medium mixing bowl, combine cream cheese and marshmallow crème at medium speed until blended and fluffy. Place in a serving bowl, cover with plastic wrap and refrigerate or chill in cooler until ready to serve. Serve with various fruits, such as apple slices, cantaloupe pieces, grapes and/or strawberries, for dipping.

Raw Veggie Dip

Makes 12 servings

**1 C. mayonnaise
1/2 C. sour cream
1 tsp. Italian-style
    dressing mix
1/8 tsp. curry powder
1 T. dried onion flakes**

**1 T. dried parsley flakes
1 1/2 tsp. lemon juice
1/4 tsp. salt
1/2 tsp. Worcestershire
    sauce**

In a medium bowl, combine mayonnaise, sour cream, Italian-style dressing mix, curry powder, dried onion flakes, dried parsley flakes, lemon juice, salt and Worcestershire sauce. Place in a serving bowl, cover with plastic wrap and refrigerate or chill in cooler until ready to serve. Serve with various sliced vegetables for dipping.

BEER CHEESE SPREAD WITH A KICK

Makes 2 cups

1 (8 oz.) pkg. shredded
    Cheddar cheese
1 (4 oz.) pkg. cream
    cheese, softened
1/3 C. beer

1 tsp. Worcestershire sauce
1 tsp. chili powder
1/2 tsp. ground mustard
1/4 tsp. cayenne pepper
1 tsp. dried parsley flakes

In a blender or food processor, combine shredded Cheddar cheese, cream cheese, beer, Worcestershire sauce, chili powder, ground mustard and cayenne pepper. Process until well incorporated and smooth. Add dried parsley flakes and mix just until blended. Remove from blender and place in a serving bowl. Cover with plastic wrap and refrigerate or chill in cooler until ready to serve. Serve with various crackers.

HERBED CHEESE SPREAD

Makes 2 cups

1 (8 oz.) pkg. cream
    cheese, softened
2 cloves garlic, minced
3 green onions, chopped
1/2 tsp. prepared mustard
1/2 tsp. Worcestershire sauce

1/4 C. fresh chopped parsley
1/4 C. fresh chopped
    dillweed
1/4 C. fresh chopped basil
1/4 C. chopped black olives
2 T. lemon juice

In a medium bowl, combine above ingredients, mixing until well blended. Place in a serving bowl, cover with plastic wrap and refrigerate or chill in cooler until ready to serve. Serve with various crackers or sliced veggies.

Honey Pecan Chex Mix

Makes 18 servings

7 C. Crispix cereal
1 C. mini twist pretzels
1 C. pecan halves
1/4 C. butter or margarine

3/4 C. brown sugar
1/4 C. honey
1 tsp. vanilla

Preheat oven to 250°. In a greased 9x13" baking dish, combine Crispix cereal, mini pretzels and pecan halves. Mix until evenly incorporated and set aside. In a medium saucepan over medium heat, combine butter, brown sugar and honey. Bring mixture to a boil, stirring frequently. Let mixture boil for 5 minutes without stirring. Remove from heat and stir in vanilla. Pour mixture over cereal mixture in baking dish. Carefully toss until evenly coated. Bake in oven for 1 hour, stirring after every 15 minutes. Let mixture cool in baking dish and store in an airtight container.

DILL PICKLE SLICES

Makes 14 servings

1 (8 oz.) pkg. cream cheese, softened
2 T. mayonnaise
1 T. onion juice
1 T. minced onions
1 (1 lb.) loaf white bread, crusts trimmed
1 (22 oz.) jar baby dill pickles

In a medium bowl, combine cream cheese, mayonnaise, onion juice and minced onions. Spread an even thin layer of the cream cheese mixture over each slice of bread. Place 1 baby dill pickle in the center of each slice of bread and roll bread slice to enclose the pickle. Place pickle rolls, seam side down, in a glass baking dish. Cover and chill in refrigerator at least 8 hours. Before serving, slice each pickle roll into 1" thick slices.

BABE RUTH BARS

Makes 18 bars

1 C. peanut butter	6 C. cornflakes cereal
1 C. light corn syrup	1 C. chocolate chips
1/2 C. brown sugar	2/3 C. peanuts
1/2 C. sugar	

In a large saucepan over medium heat, combine peanut butter, corn syrup, brown sugar and sugar. Cook, stirring occasionally, until smooth. Remove from heat and immediately stir in cornflakes, chocolate chips and peanuts, mixing until evenly coated. Press mixture evenly into a greased 9x13" baking dish. Let mixture cool completely before cutting into bars.

Raspberry Oatmeal Bars

Makes 12 servings

1/2 C. brown sugar
1 C. flour
1/4 tsp. baking soda
1/8 tsp. salt

1 C. old fashioned oats
1/2 C. butter, softened
3/4 C. seedless
raspberry jam

Preheat oven to 350°. Grease an 8" square baking dish and line with aluminum foil. In a medium bowl, combine brown sugar, flour, baking soda, salt and old fashioned oats. Using a pastry blender, cut in butter until mixture is crumbly. Press 2 cups of the crumb mixture in the bottom of prepared pan. Spread raspberry jam over crumb layer to within 1/4" of the edge of the pan. Sprinkle remaining crumb mixture over top of jam layer and press down lightly with hands. Bake in oven for 35 to 40 minutes, until bars are lightly browned. Let cool before cutting into bars.

PEANUT BUTTER BLONDIES

Makes 24 servings

3 1/8 C. flour	2 1/3 C. brown sugar
1/2 tsp. baking powder	3 eggs
1 tsp. baking soda	2 tsp. vanilla
1/2 tsp. salt	3 C. peanut butter chips
1 tsp. cinnamon, optional	1 C. chopped pecans,
1 C. butter	toasted*

Preheat oven to 350°. Grease and flour a 9x13" baking dish and set aside. Into a medium bowl, sift flour, baking power, baking soda, salt and cinnamon and set aside. In a large saucepan over low heat, heat butter until melted. Stir in brown sugar, mixing until brown sugar is completely dissolved and remove from heat. Let mixture cool and mix in eggs, one at a time, beating well after each addition. Mix in vanilla. Gradually add sifted dry ingredients, a little at a time, mixing until just blended. Fold in peanut butter chips and toasted chopped pecans. Spread batter evenly into prepared pan. Bake in oven for 30 to 35 minutes. Let cool before cutting into bars.

* To toast, place chopped pecans in a single layer on a baking sheet. Bake at 350° for approximately 10 minutes or until pecans are golden brown.

THE SIDELINES

SIDES &
SALADS

APPLE CABBAGE COLE SLAW

Makes 4 servings

1/3 C. plain yogurt	2 C. diced Red Delicious
2 T. pineapple or apple juice	or Winesap apples
1/4 tsp. mustard	1 C. sliced celery
1/8 tsp. celery seed	1/2 C. thinly sliced onion
3 C. shredded cabbage	

In a large bowl, whisk together yogurt, juice, mustard and celery seed. Add shredded cabbage, diced apples, sliced celery and sliced onions. Toss gently until completely combined. Store in an airtight container and refrigerate or chill in cooler until ready to serve.

DELICIOUS BAKED BEANS

Makes 8 servings

1 lb. ground beef
1/2 C. chopped onions
1 lb. bacon, cut into pieces
1 C. ketchup
3 T. distilled vinegar

1 C. brown sugar
1 (16 oz.) can kidney
  beans, drained
2 (16 oz.) cans baked beans
  or pork n' beans

Preheat oven to 350°. In a large skillet over medium heat, brown ground beef and chopped onions until cooked throughout and drain of fat. In a separate pan over medium heat, sauté bacon pieces until cooked and crispy. Let bacon drain on paper towels. Add cooked bacon to skillet with ground beef and onions. Mix well and stir in ketchup, vinegar, brown sugar, drained kidney beans and baked beans. Cover skillet and bake mixture in oven for 1 1/2 to 2 hours.

GAME DAY
PASTA SALAD

Makes 4 to 6 servings

1 (8 oz.) pkg. uncooked
    rotini pasta
1 (8 oz.) pkg. shredded
    Monterey Jack cheese
1/2 C. shredded carrots
1 (4 oz.) can sliced black
    olives, drained

1 small bottle Italian
    salad dressing
Grated Parmesan cheese
    to taste
Italian seasoning to taste

In a medium pot of lightly salted boiling water, cook pasta until done, about 8 to 10 minutes, and drain pot. Rinse pasta under cool, running water and let drain again. In a large salad bowl, combine cooked pasta, shredded Monterey Jack cheese, shredded carrots and drained black olives. Toss until evenly incorporated and season with Italian salad dressing, grated Parmesan cheese and Italian seasoning to taste. Store in an airtight container and refrigerate or chill in cooler until ready to serve.

B.L.T. SALAD

Makes 6 servings

1 lb. bacon, cut into pieces	**3/4 C. mayonnaise**
8 C. shredded iceberg or	**1/4 C. milk**
romaine lettuce	**1 tsp. garlic powder**
2 large tomatoes, chopped	**1/4 tsp. salt**
2 C. seasoned croutons	**1/4 tsp. pepper**

In a medium skillet over medium heat, sauté bacon pieces until cooked and crispy. Let bacon drain on paper towels. In a large salad bowl, place shredded lettuce. Top with a layer of chopped tomatoes, followed by a layer of the cooked bacon. Sprinkle seasoned croutons over bacon layer. In a blender, combine mayonnaise, milk, garlic powder, salt and pepper at medium high speed until thoroughly blended. Before serving, pour dressing mixture over ingredients in bowl, but do not toss.

Fried Potatoes

Makes 4 servings

6 slices bacon, diced
6 potatoes, peeled
   and sliced
1/2 tsp. celery seed

1/2 tsp. salt
1/4 tsp. pepper
1 tsp. fresh minced parsley
1/8 tsp. paprika

In a medium skillet over medium heat, sauté diced bacon until cooked and crispy. Let bacon drain on paper towels. Place sliced potatoes in skillet with bacon drippings. Cover skillet and fry potatoes until browned and tender, turning frequently to prevent burning. Sprinkle potatoes with celery seed, salt, pepper, minced parsley and paprika. Add cooked bacon and stir until well mixed.

PARMESAN
DEVILED EGGS

Makes 6 servings

6 hard-boiled eggs
1/2 C. grated Parmesan
   cheese
1 tsp. horseradish sauce
1/2 tsp. salt
1/2 tsp. dry mustard

1/4 tsp. pepper
3 T. mayonnaise or creamy
   salad dressing
1/2 tsp. paprika
1/4 C. sliced black olives

Peel hard-boiled eggs and cut each egg in half lengthwise. Scoop out the egg yolk and place in a medium bowl. Using a fork, mash egg yolks and add grated Parmesan cheese, horseradish sauce, salt, dry mustard, pepper and mayonnaise. Mix well and spoon mixture back into hollow eggs. Garnish eggs with a sprinkle of paprika and sliced black olives.

SIMPLE CUCUMBER SALAD

Makes 10 servings

3 or 4 cucumbers	**1 C. sour cream**
1 tsp. salt	**2 T. sugar**
1 sweet onion	**1 1/2 T. distilled vinegar**

Peel cucumbers and cut into 1/4" thick slices. Place cucumber slices in a large bowl and sprinkle with salt. Cut sweet onion into thin slices and separate slices into individual rings. Place onions in bowl with cucumber. In a medium bowl, combine sour cream, sugar and distilled vinegar. Pour mixture over cucumbers and onions in bowl and toss until evenly coated. Store in an airtight container and refrigerate or chill in cooler until ready to serve.

TORTILLA SALAD

Makes 12 servings

2 heads iceberg lettuce,
   torn
4 tomatoes, diced
1 large onion, chopped
6 C. shredded Cheddar
   cheese
1 (14 1/2 oz.) pkg. corn
   tortilla chips, crushed

2 (12 oz.) bottles creamy
   Ranch salad dressing
1 (12 oz.) jar thick n'
   chunky salsa
2 lbs. ground beef

In a large bowl, combine torn lettuce, diced tomatoes, chopped onions and shredded Cheddar cheese. Add crushed tortilla chips and toss until evenly incorporated. In a large skillet over medium heat, brown ground beef until cooked throughout. Drain of fat. Before serving, add cooked ground beef to salad and toss until well incorporated. Store in an airtight container and refrigerate or chill in cooler until ready to serve.

SEASONED CHERRY TOMATOES

Makes 6 to 8 servings

1/4 C. vegetable oil
3 T. cider vinegar
1 tsp. dried parsley flakes
1 tsp. dried basil
1 tsp. dried oregano

1/2 tsp. salt
1 1/2 tsp. sugar
4 C. halved cherry
    tomatoes

In a small bowl, combine vegetable oil, cider vinegar, dried parsley flakes, dried basil, dried oregano, salt and sugar. Mix well. In a medium serving bowl, place halved cherry tomatoes. Pour oil mixture over tomatoes and gently stir until coated. Chill in refrigerator at least 2 hours. Store in an airtight container and refrigerate or chill in cooler until ready to serve.

THREE BEAN SALAD

Makes 16 servings

1 onion, thinly sliced
1 (15 oz.) can green
    beans, drained
1 lb. waxed beans,
    washed and trimmed
1 (15 oz.) can kidney beans,
    drained and rinsed

3/4 C. sugar
2/3 C. distilled vinegar
1/3 C. vegetable oil
1/2 tsp. salt
1/2 tsp. pepper
1/2 tsp. celery seed

Separate onion slices into individual rings. In a large bowl, combine drained green beans, waxed beans, kidney beans, onion slices, sugar, vinegar, vegetable oil, salt, pepper and celery seed. Toss until well mixed. Cover and chill in refrigerator at least 12 hours. Store in an airtight container and refrigerate or chill in cooler until ready to serve.

Spicy Chilled Salad

Makes 6 servings

6 large tomatoes, peeled and quartered	1 1/2 tsp. celery salt
1 green bell pepper, sliced into rings	1 1/2 tsp. mustard seed
1 red onion, sliced into rings	4 1/2 tsp. sugar
	1/8 tsp. cayenne pepper
	1/8 tsp. pepper
3/4 C. white wine vinegar	1/4 C. water
	1 large cucumber, sliced

In a large bowl, combine quartered tomatoes, green bell pepper rings and red onion rings. In a medium saucepan over medium heat, combine white wine vinegar, celery salt, mustard seed, sugar, cayenne pepper, pepper and water. Bring to a boil. Boil for 1 minute and pour over vegetables in bowl. Mix until well incorporated and refrigerate until completely chilled. Store in an airtight container and refrigerate or chill in cooler until ready to serve. Before serving, add cucumber slices and toss until well mixed.

SESAME ALMOND SALAD

Makes 6 servings

1 head Napa cabbage,
   shredded
6 green onions, minced
1/3 C. butter
1 (3 oz.) pkg. ramen
   noodles, broken

2 T. sesame seeds
1 C. slivered almonds
1/4 C. cider vinegar
3/4 C. vegetable oil
1/2 C. sugar
2 T. soy sauce

Preheat oven to 350°. In a large bowl, combine shredded cabbage and minced green onions. Cover and chill in refrigerator. To make topping, in a medium saucepan over medium heat, heat butter until melted. Add broken ramen noodles, sesame seeds and slivered almonds. Mix well and place mixture on a lightly greased baking sheet. Bake in oven, stirring often. Topping is done when ramen noodles and slivered almonds are browned. To make dressing, in a small saucepan over medium heat, combine cider vinegar, vegetable oil, sugar and soy sauce. Bring to a boil. Boil for 1 minute and remove from heat. Let dressing mixture cool. Before serving, pour dressing over cabbage and toss until evenly coated. Sprinkle topping over salad and serve.

ITALIAN PASTA SALAD

Makes 16 servings

1 (16 oz.) pkg. uncooked
   spiral pasta
3 C. halved cherry tomatoes
1/2 lb. provolone cheese,
   cubed
1/2 lb. salami, cubed
1/4 lb. sliced pepperoni,
   cut in half

1 large green bell pepper,
   cut into 1" pieces
1 (10 oz.) can black olives,
   drained
1 (4 oz.) jar pimentos,
   drained
1 (8 oz.) bottle Italian
   salad dressing

In a medium pot of lightly salted boiling water, cook pasta until done, about 8 to 10 minutes, and drain pot. Rinse pasta under cool, running water and let drain again. In a large bowl, combine cooked pasta, halved cherry tomatoes, cubed provolone cheese, cubed salami and sliced pepperoni. Add green bell pepper, drained olives and drained pimentos and toss until evenly incorporated. Pour Italian salad dressing over ingredients and toss until evenly coated. Store in an airtight container and refrigerate or chill in cooler until ready to serve.

VEGGIE PICNIC PASTA

Makes 12 servings

1 lb. uncooked shell pasta	1/4 C. prepared mustard
1 C. chopped mushrooms	2 T. mayonnaise
1 C. chopped cucumber	1/4 C. distilled vinegar
1 C. chopped broccoli	1/4 C. shredded Cheddar
1 C. sugar	cheese
3/4 C. vegetable oil	Salt and pepper to taste

In a medium pot of lightly salted boiling water, cook pasta until done, about 8 to 10 minutes, and drain pot. Rinse pasta under cool, running water and let drain again. In a large bowl, combine chopped mushrooms, chopped cucumber, chopped broccoli, sugar, vegetable oil, mustard, mayonnaise, vinegar, shredded Cheddar cheese, salt and pepper. Mix well and add cooked pasta. Toss until evenly incorporated. Chill in refrigerator for 2 to 4 hours before serving. Store in an airtight container and refrigerate or chill in cooler until ready to serve.

MUSHROOM PATE

Makes 1 (2-quart) mold

3 C. chopped onions
2 cloves garlic, minced
4 tsp. olive oil
1 lb. fresh mushrooms,
    sliced
1 tsp. dried thyme
1 tsp. dried rosemary
1 tsp. dried sage
1/2 C. herb stuffing mix

1/2 C. grated Parmesan
    cheese
1 (8 oz.) pkg. cream
    cheese, softened
2 C. ricotta cheese
1/4 C. fresh chopped
    parsley
Salt and pepper to taste

Preheat oven to 400°. In a medium saucepan over medium heat, sauté chopped onions and minced garlic in olive oil. Add sliced mushrooms, dried thyme, dried rosemary and dried sage. Sauté until mushrooms begin to soften. Remove from heat and let cool for 5 minutes. Add herbed stuffing mix. In a blender or food processor, combine grated Parmesan cheese, cream cheese and ricotta cheese. Add mushroom mixture and process until blended and smooth. Mix in salt and pepper to taste. Grease a 2-quart mold and fill with waxed paper. Spread mushroom mixture into mold. Tap filled mold down lightly on counter to release any air bubbles. Bake in oven for 1 hour and 15 minutes. Remove from oven and let cool. Release mold onto serving platter, cover with plastic wrap and refrigerate or chill in cooler until ready to serve. Serve with crackers and vegetables for dipping.

EASY HERBED POTATOES

Makes 4 to 6 servings

2 T. olive oil
1 T. balsamic vinegar
1 tsp. garlic salt
1 tsp. dried rosemary
1/4 tsp. pepper

2 small Vidalia onions,
   cut into wedges
3 large carrots, sliced
   diagonally
2 red potatoes, chopped

Preheat grill to high heat or oven to 400°. In a 9x13" metal baking dish, combine olive oil, balsamic vinegar, garlic salt, dried rosemary and pepper. Add onion wedges, carrot slices and chopped potatoes. Toss until evenly coated. Bake in oven for 40 minutes or until vegetables are tender, or place baking dish directly over grill. Cover grill and cook, turning occasionally, until vegetables are tender.

DILL POTATO SALAD

Makes 4 to 6 servings

4 C. diced potatoes	1/4 tsp. pepper
1 C. chopped celery	1/2 tsp. dried dillweed
3 green onions, sliced	3/4 C. sour cream
3 T. vinegar	2 dill pickles, chopped
3 T. vegetable oil	1 tomato, cut into wedges
1/4 tsp. salt	

In a large pot of lightly salted water over medium heat, place diced potatoes. Bring to a boil and cook until potatoes are tender but still firm, about 15 minutes. Drain potatoes and let cool. In a large bowl, combine cooked potatoes, chopped celery and sliced green onions. In a small bowl, combine vinegar, vegetable oil, salt, pepper and dried dillweed. Mix well and pour over ingredients in bowl. Toss gently until evenly coated. Chill in refrigerator overnight. Before serving, stir in sour cream and chopped dill pickles. Garnish with tomato wedges. Store in an airtight container and refrigerate or chill in cooler until ready to serve.

AMAZING FRUIT SALAD

Makes 4 servings

1 red apple, cored
  and chopped
1 Granny Smith apple,
  cored and chopped
1 nectarine, pitted and
  sliced

2 stalks celery, chopped
1/2 C. dried cranberries
1/2 C. chopped walnuts
1 (8 oz.) carton lemon
  yogurt

In a large bowl, combine chopped red apple, chopped Granny Smith apple, sliced nectarine, chopped celery, dried cranberries and chopped walnuts. Mix until well incorporated. Spoon yogurt over fruit mixture and toss until evenly coated. Store in an airtight container and refrigerate or chill in cooler until ready to serve.

WHIPPED CRANBERRY BLEND

Makes 12 servings

4 C. ground raw cranberries
1 (16 oz.) pkg. miniature marshmallows
1 C. sugar

1 pint heavy whipping cream
2 C. apples, peeled, cored and finely chopped
1/2 C. walnuts

In a large bowl, combine ground cranberries, miniature marshmallows and sugar. Cover and chill in refrigerator at least 8 hours. In a medium mixing bowl, beat heavy cream until soft peaks form. Before serving, mix finely chopped apples and walnuts into cranberry mixture. Fold in whipped cream and mix until well blended. Store in an airtight container and refrigerate or chill in cooler until ready to serve.

GET FIRED UP

GRILLED
FOODS

Beer 'N' Brats

Makes 12 servings

3 (12 oz.) cans beer,
    any kind
2 1/4 C. water
12 uncooked bratwurst
2 tsp. minced garlic

1 tsp. brown sugar
2 onions, sliced
Salt and pepper to taste
12 brat buns
Mustard

In a medium saucepan over medium heat, place beer, water, bratwurst, minced garlic, brown sugar, sliced onions, salt and pepper. Mix and cook until liquid begins to boil. Reduce heat, cover and let cook for 25 minutes, until brats are cooked throughout. Strain onions from cooking liquid and reserve. Place onions and brats in airtight containers and chill in refrigerator or in cooler until ready to prepare. At the tailgate, preheat grill to medium high heat and cover a section of the grate with aluminum foil. Place brats over grill and cook until fully browned. Warm reserved onions by placing on aluminum foil section of the grill. To serve, place 1 brat on each bun and top with mustard and some of the heated onions.

Spicy Tailgater's Pockets

Makes 8 servings

1 pkg. McCormick Grill
    Mates Spicy Caribbean
    marinade
1/4 C. water
2 T. pineapple or orange
    juice
1 T. brown sugar
1 T. vinegar

1 lb. kielbasa, cut into
    1/4" slices
1 large red bell pepper,
    cut into strips
1 medium onion,
    cut into slices
1 pkg. pita bread or
    burrito-style tortillas

Preheat grill to medium high heat. In a small bowl, combine Spicy Caribbean marinade, water, pineapple juice, brown sugar and vinegar. Mix well and set aside. Cut aluminum foil into four 18" squares. Place an even amount of the kielbasa slices, red bell pepper strips and onion slices in the center of each aluminum foil square. Roll aluminum foil to enclose the ingredients and fold up one end, leaving one end open. Divide marinade evenly among packets and seal packets by folding down remaining open end of aluminum foil. Shake packets to coat mixture inside. Place packets on preheated grill and cook for 45 minutes, turning once. Carefully remove packets from grill and open one end. Let mixture cool for 2 to 3 minutes while letting the steam escape. To serve, divide grilled mixture into four pita bread pockets or spoon onto tortillas.

CAJUN GRILLED POTATO WEDGES

Makes 4 to 6 servings

3 large russet potatoes
   with peel, washed
   and scrubbed
1/4 C. olive oil
2 cloves garlic, minced
1 tsp. salt

1 tsp. paprika
1/2 tsp. dried thyme
1/2 tsp. dried oregano
1/4 tsp. pepper
1/8 to 1/4 tsp. cayenne
   pepper

Preheat grill to medium high heat. Place potato wedges in a large bowl and add olive oil, tossing until coated. Add minced garlic, salt, paprika, dried thyme, dried oregano, pepper and cayenne pepper. Mix together until potato wedges are completely covered. Divide potato wedges onto 2 or 3 large sheets of aluminum foil. Fold the foil to enclose potatoes in packets and place packets on grill. Grill for 40 minutes, checking that potatoes have softened. Once potatoes have softened slightly, remove packets from grill. Carefully open packets and remove wedges from aluminum foil. Discard aluminum foil. Place wedges on their sides on grill. Cover grill and cook wedges for 15 to 20 minutes, until potatoes are browned and tender.

GRILLED CORN ON THE COB

Makes 4 servings

4 ears of corn
1 1/2 T. butter, melted
1/2 tsp. ground cumin

1/4 tsp. chili powder
1 tsp. fresh chopped
cilantro

Preheat grill to medium heat. Pull back husks from ears of corn, leaving the husks attached. Remove 1 strip of husk from the inner side of each ear of corn and set aside. In a small bowl, combine melted butter, ground cumin, chili powder and chopped cilantro. Brush melted butter mixture onto corn. Bring husks up to cover corn and tie husks together with reserved strips of husk. Place corn cobs on the hot grate and grill for 20 to 30 minutes, turning corn occasionally.

CHICKEN SALAD BOATS

Makes 18 rolls

4 pkgs. of about 20 precooked chicken tenders
18 hard rolls
3 C. finely chopped celery
1 medium onion, finely chopped

4 T. mayonnaise
1 large bottle Italian dressing
Salt and pepper to taste
18 slices provolone cheese

Preheat grill to medium heat and cover the grate with aluminum foil. Grill chicken tenders until heated throughout, remove from grill and cut into small pieces. Meanwhile, hollow out hard rolls by cutting a hole in the top of each roll and pulling out the bread. Do not hollow rolls completely, but leave bottom intact to make a boat shape. In a medium bowl, combine chicken tender pieces, chopped celery, chopped onion, mayonnaise, Italian dressing, salt and pepper. Mix well and spoon mixture into hollowed hard rolls. Place hard rolls in a metal 9x13" baking dish. Place 1 slice of provolone cheese over each roll in baking dish. Place baking dish over heated grill until cheese melts and rolls are slightly browned. Remove from grill and serve warm.

TOMATO SALAD ON THE GRILL

Makes 6 to 8 servings

1 T. olive oil
1 T. fresh lemon juice
2 cloves garlic, minced
3 dashes Worcestershire
    sauce
1/2 C. fresh chopped basil

5 large ripened tomatoes,
    quartered
Salt and pepper to taste
1/2 loaf crusty bread,
    torn into pieces

Preheat grill to medium high heat and cover the grate with aluminum foil. In a small bowl, whisk together olive oil, lemon juice, minced garlic and Worcestershire sauce. Mix in chopped basil and set aside. In a medium bowl, combine quartered tomatoes, salt and pepper. Drizzle additional olive oil over aluminum foil on grill. Turn tomatoes out onto aluminum foil on grill and heat, turning frequently, until browned. In a medium bowl, toss together grilled tomatoes and chopped basil mixture. Season with additional salt and pepper to taste. Serve tomato salad with pieces of crusty bread for dipping.

SALMON SKEWERS

Makes 12 servings

1 lb. skinless salmon filet
12 wooden skewers,
   soaked in water
1/4 C. soy sauce
1/4 C. honey
1 T. rice vinegar

1 tsp. fresh minced
   gingerroot
1 clove garlic, minced
Pinch of pepper
12 lemon wedges

Preheat grill to medium high heat and lightly oil the grate. Slice salmon filet lengthwise into 12 long strips and thread each strip on a soaked wooden skewer. Place skewers in a shallow baking dish. In a medium bowl, whisk together soy sauce, honey, vinegar, minced gingerroot, minced garlic and pepper. Pour mixture over skewers in baking dish and let marinate at room temperature for 30 minutes. Pour remaining marinade into a small saucepan. Place saucepan over grill and bring mixture to a simmer. Thread 1 lemon wedge onto the end of each skewer. Place marinated skewers over heated grill and cook for 4 minutes on each side, brushing often with simmering marinade mixture. Salmon is done when it flakes easily with a fork.

LIME MARINATED STEAK

Makes 4 servings

1/4 C. vegetable oil
6 dried chili peppers,
  cut into strips
1 C. coarsely chopped onion
1 1/2 tsp. fresh chopped
  garlic
1/2 C. beef broth

2 T. fresh lime juice
2 tsp. cumin seed
1 1/2 tsp. salt
1 tsp. brown sugar
4 New York steaks,
  tenderized
2 limes

In a medium skillet over medium low heat, combine vegetable oil, chili pepper strips, chopped onion and chopped garlic and sauté until onion is tender. Pour onion mixture in a blender and add beef broth, lime juice, cumin seed, salt and brown sugar. Process until blended. Place tenderized steaks in a large ziplock bag and pour half of the marinade over steaks in bag and seal. Place remaining marinade in an airtight container. Place bags with steak and container with remaining marinade in refrigerator or cooler until ready to prepare. Preheat grill to medium heat. Place steaks over grill and baste with reserved marinade. Grill to desired doneness. Before serving, brush with additional marinade and generously squeeze lime juice over cooked steaks.

THE CHEDDAR BURGER

Makes 4 servings

1 lb. ground beef
1/3 C. steak sauce, divided
4 (1 oz.) slices Cheddar
　cheese
1 medium onion, cut into
　strips

1 medium green or red bell
　pepper, cut into strips
1 T. butter or margarine
4 hamburger buns, split
4 slices tomato

Preheat grill to medium high heat. In a medium bowl, combine ground beef and 3 tablespoons steak sauce. Mix lightly but thoroughly. Divide mixture into 4 equal parts. Shape each part into a burger, enclosing one slice of Cheddar cheese inside each burger and set aside. Place a skillet on the hot grate and cook onions and bell pepper strips in butter, heating until vegetables are tender. Stir in remaining steak sauce and keep warm. Place burgers on hot grate. Cook burgers over grill for 8 to 10 minutes, turning once, until thoroughly cooked to desired doneness. Remove burgers from grate and place burgers on buns. Top each burger with a tomato slice and some of the cooked onions and peppers.

ITALIAN SAUSAGE & PEPPERS

Makes 4 servings

1/2 C. olive oil
1/4 C. red wine vinegar
2 T. fresh chopped parsley
1 T. dried oregano
2 cloves garlic, crushed
1 tsp. salt
1 tsp. pepper

4 hot or sweet Italian
    sausage links
1 large onion, sliced into
    rings
1 large red bell pepper,
    sliced into quarters

In a small bowl, combine olive oil, vinegar, fresh chopped parsley, dried oregano, crushed garlic, salt and pepper. Place sausages, sliced onions and red bell peppers in a large ziplock bag and pour marinade over ingredients in bag. Close bags and place in refrigerator or cooler until ready to prepare. Prehcat grill to medium heat. Place a heavy skillet over heated grill. Empty contents of bag into skillet and heat, covered, about 4 to 5 minutes. Continue to grill until sausages are cooked throughout. To serve, spoon cooked sausages and some of the onions and peppers onto each serving plate.

CHEESE STUFFED BRATS

Makes 5 servings

5 fully cooked bratwurst
1/4 C. shredded Monterey
   Jack cheese
2 green onions, thinly sliced
5 slices bacon

5 French-style rolls or brat
   buns
Ketchup, mustard, chopped
   onions and/or relish,
   optional

Preheat grill to medium heat. Cut a 1/2" slit lengthwise in each bratwurst. Insert an even amount of the shredded Monterey Jack cheese and sliced green onions into the slit in each bratwurst. Wrap 1 slice of bacon around each bratwurst to enclose the green onions and cheese. Secure bacon slice with toothpicks. Place bratwursts, cut side up, over grill and heat for 5 to 10 minutes, until bacon is crisp and cheese is melted. Place brats in buns and, if desired, top with ketchup, mustard, chopped onions and/or relish.

SEASONED PORK RIBS

Makes 4 servings

1 T. chili powder
1 T. dried parsley flakes
2 tsp. onion powder
2 tsp. garlic powder
2 tsp. dried oregano

2 tsp. paprika
2 tsp. pepper
1 1/2 tsp. salt
4 lbs. pork spareribs,
    cut into 4 racks

In a small bowl, combine chili powder, dried parsley flakes, onion powder, garlic powder, dried oregano, paprika, pepper and salt. Mix well and rub over ribs. Cover ribs and let marinate in refrigerator for 2 to 8 hours. Preheat oven to 350° and place ribs in a shallow roasting pan. Bake ribs in oven for 30 minutes. At the tailgate, preheat grill to medium heat. Place ribs over grill and heat for 10 minutes, brushing frequently with BBQ Sauce (recipe below). Continue to grill until ribs are tender.

BBQ SAUCE

Makes 3 1/2 cups

3 C. prepared barbecue sauce
1/4 C. cider vinegar
1/4 C. honey

2 tsp. onion powder
2 tsp. garlic powder
Dash of hot pepper sauce

In a medium bowl, whisk together above ingredients until well mixed.

HOT GARLIC BREAD

Makes 16 servings

1 C. butter	Sea salt and pepper to taste
5 1/2 T. minced garlic	Dash of Worcestershire
2 1/2 T. crumbled blue	sauce
cheese	1 thin baguette, cut into
3 1/2 T. mixed herbs	thick slices
1 T. crushed red pepper	
flakes	

Preheat grill to high heat. Place a medium saucepan over grill. Place butter in saucepan until melted and stir in minced garlic, crumbled blue cheese, mixed herbs, red pepper flakes, sea salt, pepper and Worcestershire sauce. Mix well and heat until mixture is completely melted. Dunk baguette slices in melted mixture to coat both sides. Place coated baguette slices over grill and toast for 1 minute on each side, brushing with any remaining melted mixture.

MINI ONION BLOSSOMS

Makes 4 servings

4 large sweet onions
6 T. butter, divided

Garlic salt to taste
Salt and pepper to taste

Preheat grill to high heat. Peel the outer skin from each onion and cut each onion into quarters, keeping each onion together. Place 1 1/2 tablespoons butter and desired amount of garlic salt in the center of each onion. Wrap each onion in a double layer of aluminum foil. Place wrapped onions directly on the grill and cook for 30 to 45 minutes. Carefully remove onions from grill. Using a hot pad or oven mitt, slowly unwrap onions and season with salt and pepper to taste.

BUFFALO DRUMSTICKS

Makes 4 servings

8 large chicken drumsticks
3 T. hot pepper sauce
1 T. vegetable oil
1 clove garlic, minced
1/4 C. mayonnaise
3 T. sour cream

1 1/2 T. white wine vinegar
1/4 tsp. sugar
1/3 C. crumbled blue
   cheese
Celery sticks

Place chicken drumsticks in a large ziplock bag. In a small bowl, combine hot pepper sauce, vegetable oil and minced garlic. Pour mixture over chicken in bag. Marinate chicken in refrigerator at least 1 hour or up to 24 hours, turning occasionally. To make blue cheese dressing, combine mayonnaise, sour cream, white wine vinegar and sugar. Mix well and stir in crumbled blue cheese. Store dressing and celery sticks in airtight containers until ready to serve. At the tailgate, preheat grill to high heat. Remove chicken from bag and discard the marinade. Place chicken on grate and grill, covered, for 25 to 30 minutes, turning 3 to 4 times during grilling time. Chicken is done when it is tender and no longer pink in the middle. Serve drumsticks with blue cheese dressing and celery sticks.

VEGGIES ON THE BARBIE

Makes 4 servings

8 cherry tomatoes, halved
1 1/2 C. corn kernels
1 sweet red pepper, sliced
   diagonally
1/2 medium green pepper,
   sliced diagonally

1 small onion, sliced
1 T. fresh chopped basil
1/4 tsp. grated lemon peel
Salt and pepper to taste
1 T. plus 1 tsp. butter,
   cut into pieces

Preheat grill to medium heat. In a large bowl, combine halved cherry tomatoes, corn, red and green pepper slices, onion slices, fresh chopped basil, lemon peel, salt and pepper. Gently toss until well mixed. Cut two 12" square pieces of aluminum foil. Divide vegetable mixture in half and place each half in the center of one aluminum foil piece. Dot pieces of butter over vegetables and fold up sides of aluminum foil to make a pyramid. Twist corners together at the top to seal the packet. Place packets on grill and cook for 15 to 20 minutes, or until vegetables are tender. Season with additional salt and pepper before serving.

THE AMERICAN BURGER

Makes 4 servings

1 1/2 lbs. ground beef	**1 tsp. salt**
2 tsp. Worcestershire sauce	**1 tsp. pepper**
2 T. fresh chopped parsley	**4 hamburger buns, split**
2 tsp. onion powder	**Ketchup, mustard, chopped**
1 tsp. garlic powder	**onions, relish, optional**

Preheat grill to medium heat. In a medium bowl, combine ground beef, Worcestershire sauce, chopped parsley, onion powder, garlic powder, salt and pepper. Mix lightly but thoroughly. Shape mixture into four burgers, each about 1/2" thick. Place burgers on hot grate. Cook burgers over grill for 8 to 10 minutes, turning once, until thoroughly cooked to desired doneness. Remove burgers from grate and place burgers on buns. If desired, garnish burgers with ketchup, mustard, chopped onions and/or relish.

GRILLED TEQUILA CHICKEN

Makes 4 servings

4 boneless, skinless chicken
   breasts
1/3 C. lime juice
2 T. jalapeno pepper jelly
2 T. fresh chopped cilantro

2 T. tequila
2 T. olive oil
1 tsp. fresh minced garlic
1/4 tsp. salt
1/4 tsp. pepper

Rinse chicken breasts and pat dry. Arrange chicken breasts in an 8" square baking dish and set aside. In a small bowl, combine lime juice, jalapeno pepper jelly, fresh chopped cilantro, tequila, olive oil, minced garlic, salt and pepper. Mix well and pour over chicken in baking dish. Cover baking dish and let marinate in refrigerator for 2 to 8 hours. At the tailgate, preheat grill to medium high heat. Place marinated chicken over grill and heat until chicken is cooked throughout.

BLUEBERRY RHUBARB CRUMBLE

Makes 6 servings

3 C. fresh or frozen
   blueberries
2 C. fresh or frozen diced
   rhubarb
1/2 C. sugar
1/4 C. plus 2 T. flour,
   divided

1/2 C. quick cooking oats
1/2 C. brown sugar
1/4 tsp. nutmeg
1/4 tsp. cinnamon
1/4 C. butter or
   margarine
Whipped topping, optional

In a medium saucepan over medium heat, combine blueberries, rhubarb, sugar and 2 tablespoons flour. Cook, stirring constantly, until bubbly and thickened. Pour mixture into an 8" square metal or foil baking pan and set aside. To make topping, in a medium bowl, combine oats, brown sugar, remaining 1/4 cup flour, nutmeg and cinnamon. Mix well and, using a pastry blender, cut in butter until mixture resembles coarse crumbs. Sprinkle topping mixture over fruit mixture in baking dish. Cover pan tightly with aluminum foil. At the tailgate, preheat grill to medium heat. Place metal or foil pan over grill and heat for 20 to 25 minutes, or until topping is lightly browned. If desired, serve warm with whipped topping.

SPIKE IT!

COCKTAILS
& OTHER
FUN DRINKS

BLOODY MARY

Makes 2 servings

6 oz. tomato juice
2 oz. vodka
1 to 2 dashes Tabasco sauce
1 tsp. lime juice
Dash of Worcestershire
    sauce
1 tsp. horseradish

1/4 tsp. lemon pepper
1/8 tsp. Creole seasoning
    or salt
1/8 tsp. pepper
Ice
2 long celery stems

In a pitcher, combine tomato juice and vodka. Mix well and stir in Tabasco sauce, lime juice, Worcestershire sauce, horseradish, lemon pepper, Creole seasoning and pepper among the two glasses. Place ice in two tall glasses and pour Bloody Mary over ice in glasses. Garnish each glass with a long celery stem.

SCREWDRIVER

Makes 1 serving

Ice   **1 1/2 oz. orange juice**
1 1/2 oz. vodka

Fill a cocktail shaker with ice and add vodka and orange juice. Shake until well mixed. Strain cocktail into glass.

TEQUILA SUNRISE

Makes 1 serving

Crushed ice   **1 1/2 tsp. grenadine syrup**
1 1/2 oz. tequila   **Orange slice, optional**
1/2 C. orange juice   **Maraschino cherry,**
                             optional

Fill a tall glass with crushed ice. Pour tequila and orange juice over ice and stir. Add grenadine, but do not stir. If desired, garnish with an orange slice and maraschino cherry. Stir before drinking.

MIMOSAS

Makes 2 quarts

**1 (.75 liter) bottle
champagne, chilled**

**1 quart orange juice
Ice**

Before serving, in a large pitcher, combine chilled champagne and orange juice. Stir lightly and pour over ice in glasses.

CHOCOLATE MARTINI

Makes 1 serving

**Ice
3 oz. vodka
1/2 oz. chocolate liqueur**

**Chocolate curls for garnish,
optional**

Fill a cocktail shaker with ice, vodka and chocolate liqueur. Shake until well mixed. Strain cocktail into glass. If desired, garnish with chocolate curls.

LEMON BEER PUNCH

Makes 15 to 20 servings

1 (30 pack) light beer   **1 container pink lemonade**
1 (750 ml.) bottle vodka   **mix (to make 8 qts.)**

Fill a larger cooler jug half way with ice. Into jug, pour cans of light beer. Add vodka and pink lemonade mix and stir well.

TEXAS SANGRIA

Makes 2 quarts

2 C. Burgundy red wine   **2 C. brandy**
1 C. sugar   **1 (12 oz.) can club soda**
1 C. lemon juice   **Ice**
1 C. orange juice

In a large pitcher, combine red wine, sugar, lemon juice, orange juice, brandy and club soda. Mix until sugar is completely dissolved. To serve, pour over ice in glasses.

AMARETTO SOUR

Makes 1 serving

Ice   1 1/2 C. Squirt or
1 1/2 oz. amaretto   lemon-lime soda

Fill a cocktail shaker with ice, amaretto and soda. Shake until well mixed. Strain cocktail into glass.

BAHAMA MAMA

Makes 1 serving

Ice   1/2 C. orange juice
1 1/2 oz. coconut rum   1/2 C. pineapple juice
1/2 oz. triple sec   Dash of grenadine syrup
Splash of cream of coconut
    liqueur

Fill a cocktail shaker with ice, coconut rum, triple sec, cream of coconut liqueur, orange juice and pineapple juice. Shake until well mixed. Strain cocktail into glass. Garnish with a dash of grenadine.

THE AMERICAN FLAG

Makes 1 shooter

1/2 oz. grenadine syrup   **1/2 oz. blue Curacao**
1/2 oz. half n' half

In a shot glass, pour layers of grenadine, half n' half and blue Curacao. Shoot the drink or sip slowly to enjoy the flavor of each layer.

BERMUDA ROSE

Makes 1 serving

Ice   **1/4 oz. apricot brandy**
1 1/4 oz. gin   **1/4 oz. grenadine syrup**

Fill a cocktail shaker with ice, gin and apricot brandy. Shake until well mixed. Strain cocktail into glass. Garnish with grenadine.

HODGE-PODGE PUNCH

Makes 15 to 20 servings

Crushed ice
**1 (750 ml.) bottle Bacardi
    151 rum**
1 (750 ml.) bottle vodka
**4 (46 oz.) cans pineapple
    juice, shaken**

20 oz. Sprite
3 oz. grenadine syrup
Gummi worms, optional

Fill a large 2 to 3 gallon cooler jug half way with ice. Add rum, vodka, pineapple juice, Sprite and grenadine to jug and mix well. If desired, mix in gummi worms. To serve, ladle punch into glasses.

MIDORI PUNCH

Makes 15 to 20 servings

Ice
1 (700 ml.) bottle Midori
1 (700 ml.) bottle vodka
2 C. lemonade
2 C. club soda

Honeydew melon balls
1 kiwi, peeled and cut
   into slices
1 orange, cut into slices

Fill a large 2 to 3 gallon cooler jug half way with ice. Add Midori, vodka, lemonade and club soda to jug and mix well. Carefully mix in honeydew melon balls, kiwi slices and orange slices. To serve, ladle punch into glasses.

Havana Cocktail

Makes 1 serving

Ice
1 1/4 oz. pineapple juice

3/4 oz. rum
Dash of lemon juice

Fill a cocktail shaker with ice, pineapple juice, rum and lemon juice. Shake until well mixed. Strain cocktail into glass.

Miami Vice

Makes 1 serving

Ice
2 oz. half n' half
2 oz. root beer

Drizzle of chocolate syrup
2 oz. cola

Fill a cocktail shaker with ice, half n' half, root beer and chocolate syrup. Shake until well mixed. Strain into a tall glass. Add cola and stir.

APPLE MARTINI

Makes 1 serving

1 part vodka
1 part apple liqueur
Salt for rim of glass

Cheddar cheese wedges,
**   optional**
Fresh apple slices, optional

Fill a cocktail shaker with ice, vodka and apple liqueur. Shake until well mixed. If preferred, garnish cocktail glasses with salt by wetting the rim of the glass with water and lightly dipping into salt. Strain martini into chilled cocktail glasses. Serve with a small Cheddar cheese wedge or a fresh apple slice.

CAPE COD

Makes 1 serving

Ice
1 1/4 oz. vodka
2 to 3 oz. cranberry juice

Splash of lime juice
Lime wedge, optional

Fill a glass with crushed ice. Pour vodka and cranberry juice over ice. Add a splash of lime juice and stir lightly. If desired, garnish with a lime wedge.

71

BUTTERED RUM CIDER

Makes 6 servings

6 C. apple cider
1/2 tsp. whole cloves
1/4 tsp. nutmeg
3 cinnamon sticks

6 T. butter
6 T. brown sugar
3/4 C. rum

In a 3-quart saucepan over medium heat, place apple cider. Bring to a boil and add whole cloves, nutmeg and cinnamon sticks. Reduce heat to low and let simmer, uncovered, for 10 minutes. Strain heated cider into a thermos jug. To serve, place 1 tablespoon butter, 1 tablespoon brown sugar and 2 tablespoons rum in each mug. Fill mugs with hot cider from jug.

Eggnog Latte

Makes 5 servings

2 C. egg nog
1 T. light rum
1 T. bourbon

1 C. hot brewed espresso
Nutmeg, optional

In a small saucepan over medium heat, heat egg nog, being careful not to boil. In a large pitcher, combine heated egg nog, rum, bourbon and brewed espresso. Stir until frothy and pour into glasses. If desired, garnish with nutmeg.

Godiva Hot Chocolate

Makes 1 serving

1 C. prepared hot chocolate
1 T. chocolate syrup

2 oz. Godiva liqueur
1 T. whipped topping

Fill a mug with prepared hot chocolate and stir in chocolate syrup and Godiva liqueur. Mix well. Garnish with whipped topping.

Champagne Punch

Makes 14 servings

2 T. sugar
4 or 5 dashes of bitters
3/4 C. brandy
2 (25.4 oz.) bottles
  champagne, chilled

Crushed ice
Orange slices

In the bottom of a medium cooler jug, dissolve sugar and bitters. Mix in brandy and then chilled champagne. Add crushed ice and gently stir. Garnish with orange slices.

CITRUS HOT COCOA

Makes 1 quart

1 C. half n' half
2 C. milk
1/2 C. pulp-free orange
    juice
Strips of orange peel

6 oz. bittersweet chocolate,
    finely chopped
1/3 C. Grand Marnier
    liqueur
Whipped topping

In a large saucepan over medium heat, combine half n' half, milk, orange juice and orange peel. Heat slowly and bring to a low boil. In a measuring cup, combine 2 cups of the heated milk mixture and the chopped chocolate. Whisk briskly until chocolate is melted. Return chocolate mixture to saucepan. Discard strips of orange peel and stir in Grand Marnier liqueur. Mix well and pour into a thermos jug. At tailgate, pour hot cocoa into mugs and garnish with whipped topping.

WHITE MINT HOT CHOCOLATE

Makes about 15 servings

12 C. milk	**1/4 tsp. salt**
9 oz. white chocolate,	**1 1/2 C. peppermint**
chopped	**Schnapps, optional**
1 C. crushed candy canes	**Whipped topping**
or peppermint candies	

In a large saucepan over medium heat, place milk. Bring milk to a simmer, reduce heat to low and stir in chopped white chocolate. Mix well and stir in crushed candy canes and salt. Whisk until smooth and candy canes are completely dissolved. If desired, stir in peppermint Schnapps. Mix well and pour into a thermos jug. At tailgate, pour hot cocoa into mugs and garnish with whipped topping.

SPICED RUM COFFEE

Makes 4 servings

8 whole cloves
4 strips of orange peel
2 T. sugar
4 jiggers dark rum

3 C. strong brewed coffee
Whipped topping
Nutmeg

In each of four mugs, place 2 cloves, 1 orange peel strip, 1 1/2 teaspoons sugar and 1 jigger rum. Mix well and let stand for 5 minutes. Divide strong brewed coffee evenly into mugs and stir until sugar is completely dissolved. Garnish with whipped topping and a sprinkle of nutmeg.

Café Maria

Makes 2 servings

1/4 oz. Irish Cream liqueur
1/4 oz. Kahlua liqueur
1/4 oz. amaretto
5 oz. hot brewed coffee

Cinnamon to taste
2 T. whipped topping
Grated chocolate
2 cinnamon sticks

In a pitcher, combine Irish Cream liqueur, Kahlua, amaretto, hot brewed coffee and cinnamon. Mix well and pour into 2 mugs. Garnish each serving with whipped topping, grated chocolate and 1 cinnamon stick.

Sweet Tart

Makes 1 shooter

Ice
1 oz. vodka

1 oz. Red Bull drink

Fill a cocktail shaker with ice, vodka and Red Bull. Shake until well mixed. Strain into a shot glass and serve.

HOT RUM CIDER

Makes 30 servings

**1 (1.75 liter) bottle spiced
   rum**
3 gallons apple cider
Cinnamon to taste

Nutmeg to taste
12 cinnamon sticks
Whipped topping

In a large jug, combine spiced rum, apple cider, cinnamon, nutmeg and cinnamon sticks. Mix well and let sit overnight. At tailgate, stir until well mixed and heat in a large metal pot over grill, being careful not to boil. Ladle cider into mugs and garnish with whipped topping.

IRISH COFFEE

Makes 1 serving

2 tsp. sugar
1 jigger Irish whiskey

1 C. hot brewed coffee
1 T. whipped topping

In a mug, combine sugar and whiskey, stirring until sugar is completely dissolved. Pour coffee over sugar and mix well. Garnish with whipped topping.

FRUITY RUM PUNCH

Makes 15 to 20 servings

1 (6 oz.) can frozen orange
    juice concentrate
1 (6 oz.) can frozen pineapple
    juice concentrate
1 1/2 C. rum

1/3 C. banana liqueur
1 dash grenadine syrup
1 orange, sliced into rounds
1 lime, sliced into rounds
1 lemon, sliced into rounds

In separate pitchers, prepare orange juice and pineapple juice according to package directions. Pour prepared juices into a cooler jug. Stir in rum, banana liqueur and grenadine. Float slices of orange, lime and lemon on top. To serve, ladle punch into glasses.

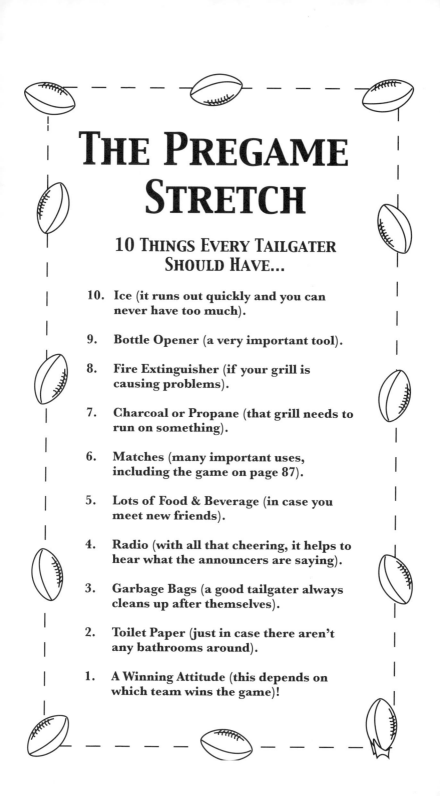

THE PREGAME STRETCH

10 THINGS EVERY TAILGATER SHOULD HAVE...

10. Ice (it runs out quickly and you can never have too much).

9. Bottle Opener (a very important tool).

8. Fire Extinguisher (if your grill is causing problems).

7. Charcoal or Propane (that grill needs to run on something).

6. Matches (many important uses, including the game on page 87).

5. Lots of Food & Beverage (in case you meet new friends).

4. Radio (with all that cheering, it helps to hear what the announcers are saying).

3. Garbage Bags (a good tailgater always cleans up after themselves).

2. Toilet Paper (just in case there aren't any bathrooms around).

1. A Winning Attitude (this depends on which team wins the game)!

GAMETRACKER

RECORD THE FINAL SCORE OF MEMORABLE GAMES ON THIS PAGE.

Date	Teams	Final Score
_____	_____ vs. _____	_____ - _____
_____	_____ vs. _____	_____ - _____
_____	_____ vs. _____	_____ - _____
_____	_____ vs. _____	_____ - _____
_____	_____ vs. _____	_____ - _____
_____	_____ vs. _____	_____ - _____
_____	_____ vs. _____	_____ - _____
_____	_____ vs. _____	_____ - _____
_____	_____ vs. _____	_____ - _____
_____	_____ vs. _____	_____ - _____
_____	_____ vs. _____	_____ - _____
_____	_____ vs. _____	_____ - _____
_____	_____ vs. _____	_____ - _____
_____	_____ vs. _____	_____ - _____
_____	_____ vs. _____	_____ - _____
_____	_____ vs. _____	_____ - _____
_____	_____ vs. _____	_____ - _____
_____	_____ vs. _____	_____ - _____
_____	_____ vs. _____	_____ - _____

THE STRATEGY

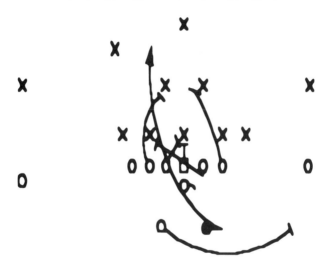

CARD GAMES
& OTHER
FRIENDLY
COMPETITION

QUICK DRAW

1 deck of cards
1 table
4 to 6 players

Each player is dealt six face-up cards in front of them at the table. The remaining cards in the deck are placed face-down in the middle of the table. The dealer turns one card at a time face up from the middle pile. When a card is turned over that has the same number or face of one of the cards in front of that player, he or she may take the card and place it with their matching card. That player should then turn over the pair of matching cards in front of them. If more that one player has a card that matches the turned-over card from the middle pile, the first one to grab the card gets to keep it. If a player mistakenly grabs a card that does not have a match, they have to draw another card from the middle pile. The first player to turn over all of the cards in front of them wins.

THE BIG BAD WOLF

1 bottle of anything drinkable
1 table
1 deck of cards
3 or more players
1 shot glass

Sit the bottle on a tall, flat surface – preferably a table. Balance the deck of cards on top of the bottle. Have each player take a turn blowing cards off the top of the deck. The person to blow the last card off the bottle has to take a shot of whatever is in the bottle. Once the deck gets down to just a few cards, the trick is to leave just one or two cards left so the person after you has no choice but to blow off the final card.

You Said It!

1 clothespin for each player
The more players the better

At the beginning of the tailgate, clip 1 clothespin onto the shirt of each player. Warn each player that if another player hears them say the words "football", "beer" or "food", that player has the right to take the faulty player's clothespin away. The winner is the person who has collected the most clothespins by the start of the game. Any words can be chosen to be the "forbidden words". Make the game more difficult by designating the forbidden words as the names or mascots of the two teams playing today.

FACES & ACES

1 deck of cards
1 table
3 to 5 players
1 drink for each player

Remove all of the Aces, Jokers and face cards from the deck. Return the Jack, Queen, King and Ace of Spades to the deck and shuffle. Lay the deck face-down in the middle of the table. The first player announces out loud how many cards he or she is going to turn over. The player can choose to turn over only between 1 and 5 cards. That player turns over the announced number of cards (between 1 and 5), one at a time. If none of those cards is the J, Q, K or A of Spades, then that player is safe and the player to the left goes next. The next player announces how many cards he or she will turn over (between 1 and 5) and turns them over, one at a time. However, that player must choose a number that is equal to or higher than the number picked by the previous person. For example, if the first player chooses to turn over 5 cards, then every player will have to turn over 5 cards until the game is over. If a player turns over the J, Q, K or A of Spades, he or she will have to take the same number of sips from their drink as the number of cards being turned over. The game is finished when the J, Q, K & A of Spades have all been turned over.

85

Baseball

4 shot glasses
Table
1 quarter
2 even teams of players
Beer

Set up the four shot glasses in a row on the table. The players must stand at the same end of the table when they are "up to bat." The first shot glass in the row represents 1st base, the second glass represents 2nd base, the third glass represent 3rd base and the fourth glass represents home base. Fill all four shot glasses with beer and decide which team is up to bat first. The players on the first team take turns bouncing the quarter off the table and into one of the shot glasses. If the quarter lands in the first glass, that person has a single. If the next person also bounces the quarter in the first glass on their turn the first player would advance and the team would now have players on 1st and 2nd base. If the quarter does not land in any shot glass, it counts as an out. When a team gets 3 outs, they have to drink the beer from all the shot glasses and the next team is up to bat. Remember to refill the shot glasses with beer. The team can continue to take turns up to bat until they have 3 outs.

Scoring:

• If the quarter lands in the last glass, it counts as a home run and the team gets 1 run.
• If a team gets multiple hits in a turn, each player advances just one base ahead. For example, if there is a player on 1st and the next player gets a double (bounces the quarter in the 2nd glass), the team would now have players on 2nd and 3rd base.
• If the team gets 3 outs with players still on base, the players do not continue from those bases when the team is up to bat again.
• The first team to get 5 runs wins!

MATCH MAKER

4 to 6 players
1 table
1 wooden matchstick
1 drink for each player

Have all players sit around the table. The players take turns spinning or tossing the matchstick in the middle of the table. When the matchstick lands, the player who has the red tip of the match pointing at him or her has to take a sip of their drink. If the match happens to land between 2 players, both players have to take a drink. When a player's drink is empty, he or she is out of the game. The last person remaining in the game is the winner.

QUEENS

1 deck of cards
1 table
4 or more players
1 drink for each player
1 tall glass

Take out all cards in deck that are lower than a 7 so that only the cards that are 7 through King remain. Take out the Aces and Jokers, as well. Shuffle the cards and place face-down in the middle of the table. The players take turns turning over 1 card from the top of the deck and laying it face-up on the table. Place the tall glass in the middle of the table. If a player turns over a King, they have to pour all of their drink into the glass.

If the player turns over a...
7 – they have to take a sip of their drink
8 – everybody takes a sip of their drink
9 – the person to that player's left takes a sip of his/her drink
10 – the person to that player's right takes a sip of his/her drink
Jack – the person directly across from that player at the table takes a sip of his/her drink
Queen – since the player is now the "Queen", they get to make up a rule*
King – the person who pulls the 4th king from the deck has to drink the contents of the glass in the middle of the table

*The Queen can make up any rules that he or she wants the rest of the team to obey. For example, if the Queen says "No one can say the word 'apple' from now on!" then the rest of the team would have to obey the Queen. The Queen can continue to make rules until a different player turns over a Queen card (now that person acts as the Queen). If someone disobeys the Queen, the Queen has the right to kick that player out of the game or make that player drink.

OH MEMORY!

1 deck of cards
1 table
2 or more players
1 drink for each player

This game is similar to the Memory matching game you may have played as a child. Lay out all cards face-down in a single layer (or in a grid pattern) on the table. The players take turns trying to make matches from the cards. For example, a 5 of Spades and a 5 of Clubs would be a match. If the player gets a match, he or she gets to assign 1 person to take a sip of his or her drink and then the player gets a chance to make another match. If the person is unsuccessful in making a match, he or she has to take a drink and their turn is over and the player to the right gets to try to make a match. The game continues until all cards have been matched up.

PLACE YOUR BETS

1 pair of dice
1 table
2 or more players

Designate 1 player as the starting bookie. The bookie calls out "Place your bets!" while the rest of the team announces out loud what number they think will be rolled. Each player has to choose a different number between 2 and 12. The bookie rolls the dice on the table. The person who has guessed right doesn't have to drink and that person becomes the next bookie. However, the players who have guessed wrong have to take a sip of their drink. If no one has guessed right, everyone takes a drink and the original bookie starts another round.

MAGIC DICE

2 or more players
1 die for each player
1 table
1 drink for each player

Designate 1 player as the announcer. Give each player 1 die. Have all players roll their die on the table at the same time. While the players are rolling their die, the announcer calls out a number between 1 and 6. If anyone has rolled the number that the announcer called, they are safe and don't have to drink. All the players who have not rolled the announcer's number have to take a sip of their drink. Take turns playing as the announcer.

VARIATIONS:

• Have the announcer call out "odd" or "even" instead of a specific number. This will ensure that more people will drink on each turn.
• To slow down the game, switch the rules so that a player has to drink when their number IS called and the remaining players are safe.

CHUG THE JUG

3 to 8 players
1 table
1 deck of cards
1 large pitcher or jug
1 drink for each player

Have everyone sit in a circle around the table. Spread the cards face-down in a single layer on the table. Place the pitcher in the center of the table. Turn over 1 card as the "Chug Card." Each player takes turns turning over 1 card from the rest of the table. At each turn, the player has to pour some of his or her drink into the pitcher. If a player turns over a card that matches the Chug Card, he or she has to drink the contents of the pitcher. For example, if the Chug Card is a 9, the first person to turn over a 9 would have to drink the contents of the pitcher. As each card is turned over, leave the card face-up on the table.

FOOTBALL

1 rectangular table
Electrical tape
4 players
1 pair of dice
1 drink for each player

Make "end zones" at both ends of the table by marking off an even section with the electrical tape. Divide the four players into 2 teams. Have one team stand at each end of the table. Each team gets two chances to roll 1 of the die into the end zone. If the die lands in the end zone, the team gets the number of points that are face-up on the die and the other team has to take that many sips from their drink. For example, if Team A rolls a die into the end zone of Team B that lands face-up as a 6, Team A would get 6 points and Team B would have to take 6 sips of their drinks. If both of the die land in the end zone, the opposite team has to take double the amount of drinks showing on the dice. The first team to get 50 points wins!

93

CATEGORIES

4 or more players
1 drink for each player

This is a simple thinking game that can be played anywhere. Take turns designating a Captain. The Captain gets to choose a category and the remaining players have to name objects that fall within that category until someone cannot think of an answer. For example, if the Captain chooses "cars" as the category, the players would go around the circle naming types of cars. The first person to go blank or repeat an answer is out and the play continues with the next player. When only one person remains, that person becomes the next Captain and chooses a new category.

Some good categories are...
• Boys/Girls Names
• Types of Beers
• Countries
• Football Teams
• Colors
• Types of Trees/Flowers
• Things with Eyes

CROSS THE BRIDGE

1 deck of cards
1 table
3 or more players
1 drink for each player

Shuffle the cards and lay 10 cards face-down in a row in the middle of the table. This row is the bridge and the object of the game is to "cross" the bridge. Players take turns flipping the cards over, starting at one end of the row. If a player turns over a card with a number on it, they are safe and can flip over the next card. If the player flips over a different card, their turn is over and he or she has to drink as follows:

Jack – the player has to take 1 sip of his/her drink
Queen – the player has to take 2 sips of his/her drink
King – the player has to take 3 sips of his/her drink
Ace – the player has to take 4 sips of his/her drink
Joker – the player has to take 5 sips of his/her drink

When one player's turn is over, the cards that have been flipped over are replaced with new face-down cards and the next player tries to cross the bridge. The first person to turn over all numbered cards and cross the bridge is the winner!

95

7-11-DOUBLES

1 pair of dice
1 table
2 or more players
1 glass for each player

Players take turns rolling the pair of dice until one player rolls a combination that adds up to 7, 11 or rolls a pair of matching numbers (doubles). If a player rolls one of these numbers, that player gets to choose one of the other players in the game to drink. The chosen player has to fill his or her glass half full of beer or a drink (being sure not to touch the glass when filling it) and finish the drink before the original player can roll another combination that adds up to 7, 11 or rolls a pair of doubles. The person rolling the dice CANNOT start rolling until the person who is drinking touches the filled glass with his or her hands. If the person who is drinking does not finish the drink before the roller rolls a 7, 11 or double then the person has to pour another drink and repeat the process. If the person who is drinking finishes his or her drink before the roller can roll a 7, 11 or double then the dice are passed to the next person and the game starts again.

BUZZ!

3 or more players
1 drink for each player

Have all players sit in a circle. One person starts the game by saying the number "1". The person to the right says the number "2" and the person to their right says the number "3". Simple enough? Well it gets a little more complicated. When it is time for the player to say the number "7", instead that player has to say "Buzz" and play continues in the opposite direction. Also, whenever a player gets to a number that is a double number, such as 11, 22, 33, 44 or 55, that player instead says "Buzz" and play continues in the opposite direction. And… whenever a player gets to a number that is a multiple of 7, such as 14, 21 or 28 or a number that has a 7 in it, such as 17, 27 or 37, that player instead says "Buzz" and play continues in the opposite direction. For example, a round of play would sound like this: 1, 2, 3, 4, 5, 6, BUZZ, 8, 9, 10, BUZZ, 12, 13, BUZZ, etc. If any player mistakenly says one of the forbidden numbers instead of Buzz, he or she has to take a sip of their drink and the group starts over at 1. When the entire group has gotten to 77, the game is over!

21 ACES

5 or more players
3 pairs of dice
1 glass
Various types of beer or liqueur

Each player takes turns rolling all of the dice. The game is played by counting the "ones" that are rolled. When a player rolls a "one" (or an "Ace"), everyone says out loud "1". If a player rolls 3 ones, everyone would count out loud "1, 2, 3" in order to keep track of how many "Aces" have been rolled. The play continues until someone rolls the 7th "Ace". The person to roll the 7th "Ace" gets to decide what drink (or concoction) to pour in the glass. The person who rolls the 14th "Ace" gets to pour any amount of the chosen drink in the glass. The person who rolls the 21st "Ace" has to drink the concoction in the glass.

CONNECTIONS

1 deck of cards
4 to 10 players
1 drink for each player

Remove Jokers from the deck and shuffle the cards. Deal all cards face-down in a pile in front of each player. Don't worry about any extra cards – deal those too. The person to the left of the dealer starts by flipping over one of their cards. The next person to the left flips over one of their cards too. If the two cards have any connection (same number or same suit) then those two people have to take the same number of sips of their drinks as the sum of the two cards (face cards are worth 10 and an Ace is worth 11). If there is no connection, then the next person to the left flips over one of his or her cards. If that person can make a connection with one of the previous cards, then those two people have to drink the sum of their cards. If someone can make a connection with multiple players, then that person gets to choose who has to drink with them. Once all players have flipped over a card, the process starts again with a new person.

SPOONS

1 deck of cards
1 less spoon than the amount of players
(4 spoons for 5 players, 9 spoons for 10 players, etc.)

Remove the Jokers and shuffle the cards. The object of this game is to collect four matching cards (4 aces, 4 sevens, etc.) and to not be the person left without a spoon. Place the spoons in the middle of the table, making sure they are within grabbing distance of all players. Deal 4 cards to each player and the dealer keeps the deck. The dealer starts the game by picking up 1 card from the deck, deciding if he or she wants to keep it and passing it on. If any player decides to keep the passed card, they must discard 1 card from their hand, making sure to only have 4 cards at all times. The dealer continues passing cards around the circle. Once one player has four of a kind, he or she can grab a spoon from the pile. Once someone has grabbed a spoon from the pile, the rest of the players are free to grab a spoon. The player without a spoon is out of the game. The game continues by eliminating the player without a spoon and 1 spoon from the pile. The cards are reshuffled and dealt. The winner is the last player still in the game.

Note

This game is very exciting when the dealer passes the cards as quickly as possible and the player with four of a kind is very discreet when grabbing a spoon. Sometimes players will continue playing for quite a while before realizing there is a missing spoon.

THE SCOREBOARD

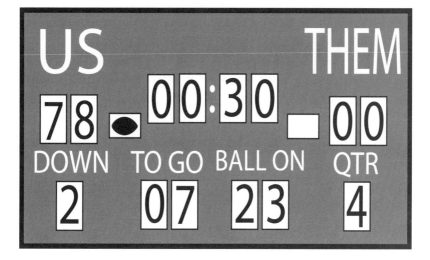

US			THEM
78	00:30		00
DOWN	TO GO	BALL ON	QTR
2	07	23	4

BEANBAGS, FOOTBALLS & FRISBEES

500

3 or more players
1 football

Designate one player as the first "thrower". Have all players except for the thrower stand in a cluster that is within throwing distance away from the thrower. The thrower holds the football and yells out a number between 50 and 500 and throws the football at the cluster of players. If one of the players catches the ball, he or she would receive the number of points that the thrower yelled out. However, if he or she drops the ball, they would lose that number of points (negative points are possible). The thrower continues to throw the ball and call out numbers. The first person to rack up 500 or more points becomes the new thrower.

FLYING BABIES

1 football
3 or more players

Designate one player as the first "thrower". Give all remaining players a different number. All remaining players cluster around the thrower. The thrower tosses the football up in the air and yells, "Baby in the air" followed by a number of one of the players. The player whose number is called has to catch the ball while all remaining players (including the thrower) scatter in all directions. As soon as the player catches the ball, he or she has to yell, "Freeze!" All remaining players have to freeze where they are. Then the player with the ball can take 3 steps in any direction. The player then tries to throw the ball at any of the other players. If the player hits another player, the hit player gets a "B". If the player throwing the ball misses another player, the throwing player gets a "B". The process goes again until one player has enough letters to spell "BABY". When any player has four letters, they are out. The last person remaining is the winner!

DOWN, DOWN, DOWN

2 or more players
1 Frisbee

Have all players stand apart but within throwing distance of each other. Toss the Frisbee back and forth until one of the players drops the Frisbee (it has to be a catch-able toss). Any player who drops the Frisbee has to play with 1 knee on the ground and the tossing continues. If a player drops the Frisbee again, he or she has to play with both knees on the ground. If a player drops the Frisbee for a third time, he or she has to play with 1 elbow on the ground and the tossing continues. If a player drops the Frisbee for a fourth time, he or she has to put both knees and both elbows on the ground and he or she is out. The last player remaining without all knees and elbows on the ground is the winner!

FRISBEE BOWLING

10 empty cans or bottles
2 or more players
1 Frisbee

Set up the empty cans or bottles on a flat piece of ground (Diagram 1). Draw a line that is 10 or more feet from the front can. Have each player take turns standing behind the line and rolling the Frisbee at the empty cans to try to knock them over. Each player gets to roll the Frisbee twice per turn and the scoring is as follows:

• 1 point for each can or bottle knocked over
• -1 point for each roll that does not knock over any cans
• If all 10 cans are knocked over in 1 roll, player gets 10 points plus 2 bonus points
• If all 10 cans are knocked over in 2 rolls, player gets 10 points plus 1 bonus point
• The first player to get 30 points is the winner!

Diagram 1

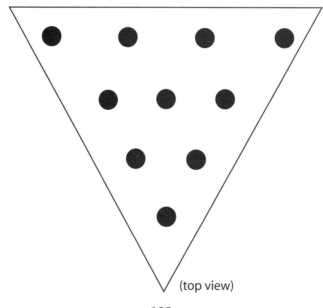

(top view)

MAKE YOUR OWN BEAN BAG TOSS

Circular saw
1 (4'x8') piece of 1/2" plywood
1 (7') piece of 1"x1" board
Yardstick
Pencil
Reciprocating saw or jigsaw
Wood glue
C-clamps
Drill
1" wood screws
Paint

Using the circular saw, cut the 4'x8' piece of plywood in half to make two 4'x4' pieces.* Set one of the 4'x4' pieces aside. Using the pencil, divide the remaining piece of 4'x4' plywood in half diagonally and saw this piece in half using the circular saw. You should now have two diagonally-cut pieces of plywood. Mark the midpoint of the 7 foot board and cut on that line to make two pieces of 3 1/2' board (Diagram 1). Mark 1, 2 or 3 holes on the front of the remaining 4'x4' board. These holes will act as the bean bag holes. Each hole should be approximately 5" to 6" in diameter. Cut out the holes with a reciprocating saw or jigsaw. Down both sides of the board, draw a line with the pencil that is 1/2" in from either edge. Turn the game board over on a flat surface and, with the pencil, mark the appropriate sides of the board with "top" and "bottom". Place one of the 3 1/2' boards along one side of the game board (not the top or the bottom), 1/2" in from the edge. Use wood glue to hold the plywood and the board together. Attach C-clamps to hold the board in place and turn the board over so the right side is up. Drill screws along the line marked 1/2" in on either side of the board. Drill 1 screw approximately every inch (Diagram 2). Turn the board over again and place remaining 3 1/2' board on the other side of the plywood piece, glue, clamp and turn over again to drill board in place. Turn the board face down again

(continued from previous page)

and place one diagonal piece along the inside of each 3 1/2' board, so that the long piece of the diagonal boards would sit flat on the ground when the bean bag toss is upright. Glue and clamp boards in place, turn over and place screw every 1" so diagonal boards are attached (Diagram 3). Reinforce the boards by drilling screws through the sides of the 3 1/2' boards and into the diagonal pieces. Sit the bean bag toss upright so the front of the board rests at an angle and paint the face of the board as desired (Diagram 4).

*(Many home improvement stores and lumber stores will cut your plywood for you at little or no charge.)

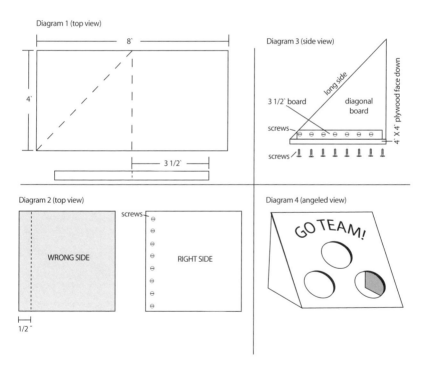

Diagram 1 (top view)

8`

4`

3 1/2`

Diagram 2 (top view)

WRONG SIDE

RIGHT SIDE

screws

1/2 ˝

Diagram 3 (side view)

long side

3 1/2` board

diagonal board

screws

screws

4' X 4' plywood face down

Diagram 4 (angeled view)

GO TEAM!

BAGG-O

2 Bean Bag Toss Boards
2 bean bags
2 or more players

Place the two bean bag toss boards approximately 20' apart on the ground facing each other. To make your own Bean Bag Toss, see directions on page 106. Divide all players onto two teams and have each team stand next to one of the bean bag boards. The two teams take turns tossing the bean bags at the other team's board. Each team gets 3 tosses per turn.

SCORING:

•   A bean bag that goes through a hole is worth 2 points.
•   A bean bag that lands on the board but does not go all the way through the hole (even if it rests partially in the hole) is worth 1 point.
•   The first team to reach 21 points is the winning team.
•   A team can cancel out the opposing team's points by gaining the same amount of points on the following turn. For example, if Team A got 6 points during one round and Team B got 6 points on their very next turn, Team A would not receive 6 points. However, Team A would now have a chance to cancel out Team B's 6 points by earning 6 points on their next turn.

Sliding Bean Bags

Chalk
Concrete parking lot or sidewalk
4 bean bags
2 or more players

Using the chalk, draw a figure that is similar to Diagram 1 on the parking lot or a nearby sidewalk. Mark each section of the figure with a different number, with the higher numbers in the smaller sections. Draw a line that is approximately 15' to 20' from the closest section of the figure. Divide all players into two teams. Have each team take turns tossing the bean bags at the figures. If a bean bag lands on the figure, they get the points of the corresponding section that most of the bean bag rests within. Each team gets to throw two bean bags per turn. When a team has thrown their two bean bags, the opposing team has a chance to knock their bean bags out of the figure. However, if they knock the other team's bean bags into a different section, the team will now get the new amount of points. For example, if Team A tosses their two bean bags into sections 25 and 30, they have 55 points for the round. But, if Team B knocks the bean bag in section 30 off the board, but knocks the bag in section 25 into section 35, Team A would now have only 35 points. Each team takes turns tossing first (offense) and tossing second (defense).

Diagram 1

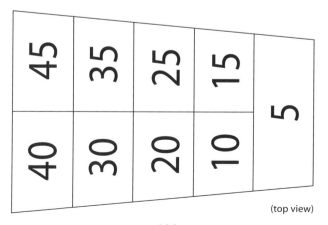

(top view)

109

Ultimate Frisbee

A large open space
An even number of players (4 or more)
1 Frisbee

Divide the open space into the playing field by designating two end zones at either end of the field. A regulation field is 40 yards x 70 yards, with end zones that are 25 yards deep.

Divide all players into two even teams. In each round of play, one teams acts as the offense and the opposing team acts as the defense. At the start of each round, both teams begin by lining up inside their respective end zones. The team that is on defense throws the Frisbee towards the team on offense. The team on offense catches the Frisbee and tries to pass it down the field toward the other team's end zone. If they reach the end zone, the team scores 1 point.

RULES:

- The Frisbee can be thrown in any direction.
- When a player has the Frisbee, they may not run, but are allowed only 2 steps to throw the Frisbee again. This person has only 10 seconds to throw the Frisbee before it is turned over to the opposing team.
- The Frisbee changes possession when a pass is not completed or is intercepted by a player on the opposing team. The Frisbee also changes possession when it is thrown out of bounds, dropped, blocked or if the thrower takes more than 2 steps or holds the Frisbee for more that 10 seconds.
- The first team to score 21 points wins.

FRISBEE BOCCE BALL

2 or more players
A large open space
1 Frisbee for each player

Divide the players into two even teams. Have one player choose an object somewhere within the playing space (a tree, a lawn chair, an empty can, a cooler, etc.). Each player takes turns trying to throw their Frisbee near the decided object. The three players who land their Frisbee closest to the object gain points for his or her team.

SCORING:

- The player with the Frisbee closest to the object gets 3 points.
- The player with the second closest Frisbee gets 2 points.
- The player with the third closest Frisbee gets 1 point.
- A player can knock another player's Frisbees farther away from the object.
- The first team to score 15 points wins.
- After each round of play, have another player pick a new object at which to throw the Frisbees.

TENNIS FRISBEE

**A large open space
2 to 4 players
1 Frisbee**

Divide the open space into a "court" by marking off an area that is approximately 30'x15' with a line dividing the middle (the net). Mark off the 2' on either side of the net as the dead zone (see Diagram 1). Empty bottles, large cones or rope make good court markers.

Have one team stand on either side of the court. The two teams take turns throwing the Frisbee onto the opposing team's side of the court. The opposing team has a chance to catch the Frisbee and throw it back to the other team's side of the court. However, if the team doesn't catch the Frisbee and it lands on the ground within their side of the court, the other team gets 1 point. If the Frisbee lands or rolls outside of the court, then no points are scored. The object of the game is to land the Frisbee on the other team's side of the court before they can catch it. If the team doesn't catch the Frisbee, but knocks it out of bounds, no points are scored. If the team drops the Frisbee within their court, the other team gets 1 point. No points are scored if the Frisbee lands in the dead zone.

Diagram 1

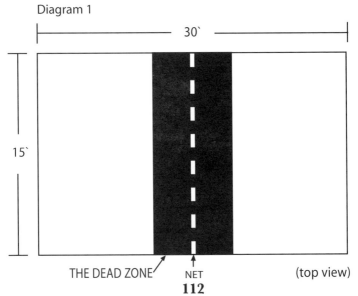

30`

15`

THE DEAD ZONE   NET   (top view)

112

PEG IN A BOTTLE

1 long piece of string
1 pencil
1 empty bottle
2 or more players
1 drink for each player

Tie one end of the string securely around the pencil. Tie the other end of the string around the waist of a player so the pencil hangs down in front of the player. Set the empty bottle on the ground in the middle of the playing area. Each player gets a chance to try to lower the pencil into the empty bottle by squatting over the bottle. However, the player can not use his or her hands to try to lower the "peg" into the bottle. The remaining players count out loud to 10. If the player can lower the peg into the bottle before the remaining players count to 10, then it is another player's turn to tie the string around his or her waist and lower the peg. However, if the player cannot lower the peg into the bottle before the remaining players count to 10, then that player has to finish their drink immediately.

Bottle Guts

8 to 12 players
1 empty bottle or can for each player
1 Frisbee for each player

Divide the players into two even teams. Have each team stand in a line facing each other with each player on one team 2' feet apart. Stand one bottle in front of each player (see Diagram 1). Each player has their own Frisbee. The object of the game is to knock over all the bottles in front of the other team before all of your own team's bottles are knocked over. Each player has to retrieve their own Frisbee after it is thrown and return back to their place behind their bottle. A player is "out" and can no longer throw his or her Frisbee once the bottle in front of that player has been knocked over. The last team with bottles still standing is the winning team!

Diagram 1

Team A				Team B	
X	•			•	X
X	•			•	X
X	•			•	X
X	•			•	X
Players	Bottle			Bottle	Players

Leave at least 2' of space between players.

POOR MAN'S
WASHER TOSS

2 or more players
2 empty coffee cans
2 large cardboard boxes
4 large metal washers
Paint

Divide the players into two even teams. Paint the washers in two different colors so there are two washers of each color. Set the two cardboard boxes approximately 15' apart on the ground. Set one empty coffee can inside each cardboard box. Have each team stand next to one of one of the cardboard boxes. The two teams take turns tossing the washers at the other team's board. Each team gets 2 tosses per turn. The scoring is as follows:

• A washer that lands in the cardboard box is worth 1 point.

• A washer that lands in the empty coffee can is worth 2 points. Each team can place the coffee can any place within their cardboard box.

• The first team to reach 21 points is the winning team.

Lion's Cub

5 or more players
1 football
1 drink for each player

Choose one player to be the first "lion". Designate something in the area to be "base" (a lawn chair, a tree, a cooler, etc.). The lion sits on the ground with the football placed right behind his or her back. The remaining players try to sneak up behind the player and steal the football (the cub) and take it back to base before they are caught by the lion. When the lion suspects there is someone trying to steal his or her cub, the lion turns around and roars at the player and immediately starts chasing him or her back to base. If the lion catches the player before that player reaches base, that player becomes the new lion. If a player can grab the football and return to base before the lion catches him or her, then the lion has to down his or her drink completely and act as the lion again. If the lion mistakenly turns around and roars when there are no players trying to steal his or her cub, then the lion has to down his or her drink completely and act as the lion once again.

INDEX
THE PREGAME MEAL

The Starting Line-Up
APPETIZERS

The Sidelines
SIDES & SALADS

Get Fired Up
GRILLED FOODS

THE PREGAME STRETCH

The Strategy
CARD GAMES & OTHER FRIENDLY COMPETITION

The Scoreboard
BEANBAGS, FOOTBALLS & FRISBEES